The Entrepreneur's Guide for Starting a Business

Connie Sparks

Author
Trainer
Educator
Consultant

Win Publishing, Castaic, CA

Published by Win Publishing
27305 W. Live Oak Rd., Ste A-421
Castaic, CA 91384
(661) 208-8229

ISBN: 978-0-9824077-1-4

Edited by
Nancy Perry

About the Author

Connie Sparks Author, Business Strategist, and Trainer is President of the Wade Institute, LLC a Business Development and Training Company established in January 2000. Wade Institute (WIN) provides an array of business planning products including access to capital to women in the business community. She is recognized as an advocate for educating and training women, promoting success, growth, and leadership. Moreover, through community partnerships she has trained more than 4,000 business owners and executives collectively throughout California.

Ms. Sparks serves as a Board of Director for the Santa Clarita Domestic Violence Center where she takes pride in creating opportunities and supporting disadvantage women and children. She is committed to building communities and the workforce. Her contribution includes serving on the Black Business Committee as a Business Relations Director, a consultant and trainer for the Santa Clarita Small Business Development Center, and an Intermediary Technical Assistant with the Small Business Administration (SBA) and Superior Financial Group.

Her background includes more than fifteen years in the business service industry, nine years in management, program development and human resources, collectively. Her education includes a degree in Business Management and Human Resource, and she holds a credential in Business Communication and Computer Applications.

Ms. Sparks's published work as an author include *The Survival Guide for African American Women, Where's The Money-Big Dollars To Do Big Business Like The Big Boys* and the *Entrepreneur's Guide to Starting a Business* just to name a few. She's been featured in various news articles circulated internationally, discussing her views on domestic violence, entrepreneurship and business development.
2002 she produced a show "Just Talk", addressing issues on relationships and minority owned small businesses. Her efforts to reach the small business community have been recognized by higher education institutions, associations, and corporate America.

She has been honored by Toastmasters International (President's Distinguished Award 2002), The For You Network- National Association of Female Executives (NAFE) (Business Woman of the Year 2006), (Best Corporate Environment Award 2006), and (Sphere of Influence Award 2007), the Los Angeles Business Journal (Women Who Make A Difference 2007, 2009), and the U.S. Small Business Administration (Home-Based Business Champion Award 2009).

Table of Contents

Introduction

I designed this book with you in mind, the serious, determined and driven entrepreneur, with a vision to be successful and prosperous.

The information provided will be very useful in other areas during your development process. The content in this booklet includes outlines and steps an entrepreneur should take when starting a new business such as how and where to apply for the appropriate licenses and permits, how to create a press release, and how to establish your home-office, opening a business bank account, and building relationships.

Also, you will find tips and guidance on how to establish your business using a step by step formula, with easy to follow instructions, which, outlines suggested tasks to be completed with approximate timelines. Some tasks maybe more complex to those with little or no experience in certain areas, therefore, timelines and benchmarks maybe shifted accordingly.

Starting a business can be challenging and overwhelming. This book was developed to ease some of that frustration and the challenges entrepreneurs encounter during the early stages of development. There's nothing worse than not knowing what to do or where to go for assistance. Not knowing causes most entrepreneurs to procrastinate or make costly mistakes in their first year of business.

According to California Census, 2002, more than 30,000 businesses register with the County Registrars office each year. Within the first two-three years in business, 80%-90% dissolve, partly due to lack of financing, lack of experience, and/or no business planning skills.

DO YOU HAVE WHAT IT TAKES?

- ❖ Are you a self-starter?
- ❖ Are you good at making decisions?
- ❖ Do you have the stamina?
- ❖ Do you have organizational skills?
- ❖ Are you self-motivated?
- ❖ Are you willing to sacrifice?
- ❖ Are you a people's person?

---

10 COMMON MISTAKES ENTRENUERS MAKE

- ❖ Not prepared
- ❖ Don't have the passion
- ❖ Don't have a business plan
- ❖ Fail to research their market
- ❖ Has no organizational skills
- ❖ Don't know their industry
- ❖ Lack of funding resources
- ❖ Bad location
- ❖ Bad partnership
- ❖ Lack of business sense

Qualifications for a Home Office Business

There are advantages to having a home office business.

1. You don't fall into the same tax bracket as storefront businesses
2. In most cases a business license is not required
3. Flexibility
4. If structured as a Corporation, you can receive the same benefits as a large Corporation.

Qualifications:
- Your home must be the principal place of business
- You must use an area of the home to conduct business
- You must conduct administrative or managerial activities in the home
- You cannot have an office suite where you conduct business, and claim to be a home-based business as well.

Step 1: Naming Your Business

#1

Selecting a name for your business may seem to be an easy task, when in fact it's one of the most challenging decisions you will come across during the development of your business.

When naming your business, take into consideration the types of products or services you will offer to consumers, what the business represents, what your primary target market is, and what's important to you about your business – i.e., customer service, quality products, a trained staff, etc. Your business and the name of your business is a reflection of who you are.

List three names you would like to use.
The name of your business:

1. _____

2. _____

3. _____

Registering Your Business/DBA

Businesses in the State of California are required to register their business names with one of the State's official business offices: the County Registrar's office located in Norwalk, CA or the Secretary of State, depending on the structure of your business.

Businesses wishing to structure their business as a Sole-Proprietor or General Partnership can register with the County Registrar's office.

Businesses interested in incorporating their business.must file with the Secretary of State.

Processes to get registered with the County Registrar's office:

After choosing a name, go to the County Registrar's web site **(www.lacounty.gov)** and follow these steps:

Step One: Select a name

Step Two: Conduct an Internet name search

Step Three: Complete the DBA registration form (print)

Step Four: Mail or drop off the application to the Registrar's office

Step Five: Run a notification in a publication for four weeks.

Note: You must run the notification within 30 days of the DBA registration date.
Up to three business names can be registered with one application for a fee of 23.00 ($23.00 for one and $4.00 for additional names). A DBA is good for a period of five years, thereafter you must renew your registration.

It will take approximately 4-8 weeks for a DBA to be effective and valid, which includes the filing and publication. Also, keep in mind, **if you do not run the publication within 30 days of the filing, your DBA becomes invalid and you will have to re-file.**

When you don't have to file a DBA:

1. If you are using the first and last name of the business owner

2. If you are incorporating the business.

Resources:
1. County Registrar- (562) 462-2177

Publications:
2. Pasadena Journal- (626) 798-3972

#3

Structuring the Business

Sole Proprietor:

- ❖ Easiest, most common, and least costly business structure.
- ❖ Can operate under your social security number.
- ❖ Have complete authority.
- ❖ Personally liable for all obligations of the business.
- ❖ Need federal id # if you will have employees.
- ❖ You pay taxes on income of the business at whatever income tax bracket you are in plus self-employment tax.
- ❖ You will file a schedule C when you file your 1040 & Schedule C or C EZ-Net profit from business.
- ❖ File (SE) Self-Employment Tax to report social security and Medicare on net profits.

General Partnership:

- ❖ Much the same as the sole proprietorship.
- ❖ Written partnership is recommended, but not required.
- ❖ Each partner is an authorized agent of the business.Partners are jointly liable for all the obligations of the business & personal assets are at risk.
- ❖ Pay taxes in much the same way as sole-proprietorships.
- ❖ File a form 1065 with the IRS when you file your personal tax returns.
- ❖ Each partner gets a schedule K1, income expenses and credits are transferred from schedule K1 to form 1040

Limited Partnership:

- ❖ Must have at least one limited partner and one general partner.
- ❖ Partners are not liable for the obligations of the partnership.
- ❖ Limited partners are only liable for the partnership's debts equal to their investment in the partnership.
- ❖ Must pay an annual tax payment of $800.
- ❖ Partnerships are required to file partnership returns.

Limited Liability Partnership:

- ❖ Provides its partners a limitation on personal liability similar to limited partnerships.
- ❖ To qualify as a limited liability partnership, all of the partners of a general partnership must be licensed to practice professional services such as accounting or law.
- ❖ Limited liability partnerships file Form 565, Partnership Return of Income.
- ❖ Can be a "fixed or at-will" term.
- ❖ Has pass through benefits.

Limited Liability Company (LLC):

- ❖ Required to file with the Secretary of State.
- ❖ Member of the LLC are not liable for obligations of the LLC.
- ❖ Have annual pretax payment.
- ❖ Suitable for partnerships.
- ❖ Limited Liability fee is considered a deductible ordinary and necessary business expense.
- ❖ $80 filing fee and $800 minimum tax obligation.
- ❖ Operating Agreement assigns authority either to the members of the LLC or to its managers.
- ❖ Economic interests are transferable, but not the voting & management interests.
- ❖ Avoid double taxation.

4

- ❖ No stock to use as incentives. May be tougher to raise capital from investors.

- ❖ Responsible for self-employment tax.

C Corporation:

- ❖ Owned by shareholders
- ❖ Shareholders are taxed on distributed dividends
- ❖ Must create bylaws
- ❖ Has limited liability
- ❖ Owners have control
- ❖ Can transfer ownership through stock sale
- ❖ Must file with SOS
- ❖ Pay taxes quarterly
- ❖ Taxed 8.84% on net income
- ❖ Pay min $800 tax
- ❖ First year $800 min tax is waived

S Corporation:

- ❖ Has limited liability
- ❖ Must create bylaws
- ❖ Limited to 100 owners
- ❖ Pay's a reduced tax on net income (1.5%)
- ❖ Has pass through benefits
- ❖ Must file with SOS
- ❖ Pay taxes quarterly
- ❖ $800 min tax

Outlining Your Business Plan

Every entrepreneur has a vision and an idea of which direction he/she wants the business to go. However, in order to properly put that vision into motion, the entrepreneur must have a plan of action.

Here is where you should take a few hours to visualize and identify the characteristics of your business. Start by jotting down your mission, goals and objectives. A mission statement consists of two sentences, describing what you do and how your customers will benefit from it.

Mission Statement: _____

_____

_____

_____

Every business no matter how small or large has a legal duty of care to consumers and its community. As a business owner you have a social responsibility to your stakeholders, which are employees, shareholders, customers, and your community. Social responsibility can be performed in many forms. However, let's focus on your community and customers. Write a social mission statement as you would a business mission statement, except focus on how you intend to give back to stakeholders, which you are committed to (community & customers).

(i.e. volunteer, have fundraisers, sponsor youth groups, donations, etc.)

Social Mission Statement: _____

_____

_____

_____

Goals:
1.
_____

2.
_____

3.
_____

Objectives:

1.
_____

2.
_____

3.
_____

Note: See Appendix Pg. 46

Step 2: *Employer's Identification Number*

#1

Apply for your Employer Identification Number (EIN). The Internal Revenue Service (IRS) provides this number to you. Even as a Sole-Proprietor you should have this number, which protects you from identity theft when dealing with suppliers, agencies, etc. An EIN is also used for businesses with one or more employees. As a Sole-Proprietor with no employees you are not required to pay related employment taxes.

Note: A Limited Liability Company (LLC) can be organized as a Sole-Proprietor or corporation. All corporations and LLCs organized, as a corporation must provide IRS with copies of Articles of Incorporation or Articles of Formation.

You can apply for your EIN online or over the phone. You will receive your identification number immediately, when applying over the phone.

Resources:
   1. IRS- (800) 829-4933 or visit www.irs.gov

EIN # _____

#2

Setting Goals for the Business

Day 1, you visualized and identified the characteristics of your business. Now, let's visualize how you'll get there.

Reflecting on your goals and objectives, what will it take for you to achieve them? Underneath each goal, write how you will achieve it.

Goal 1:

_____

1.

_____

2.

_____

3.

_____

Goal 2:

_____

1.

_____

2.

_____

3.

_____

Goal 3:

_____

1.

_____

2.

_____

3.

_____

Step 3: *Business License & Permits*

#1

Obtaining a Business License

Not all businesses require a Business License. Licensing depends on two factors 1) the City/ County where the business is located and, 2) the type of business.

Business Licenses are obtained through the City Clerk's Office. Depending on the type of business, cost for a Business License will vary.
Types of businesses that may not require a business license are: (**Check with your City Clerk's office to verify**)

1. Home based businesses

2. E-commerce businesses

3. Retail sellers who do not have a store front

4. Consultants working from home

Resource:
   1. County Clerk- (213) 974-0093 www.lacounty.gov

Obtaining a Seller's Permit for your business

If you are doing business as a retailer with sales tax, you are required to obtain a Seller's Permit from the State Board of Equalization. (Go online to find the nearest office to you at www.boe.gov)

There is no fee for this permit. As a permit holder, you will be required to report quarterly or annual sales taxes to (the) BOE. Additionally, if you are selling products in multiple locations (tradeshows, flee markets, store fronts) you must have a permit for each location.

Resource:

   1. State Board of Equalization – (818) 904-2300

Apply for State and County Certifications

Every business no matter how small or large should take advantage of all available growth opportunities. The State of California and county of Los Angeles offer small business owners the opportunity to become certified and contract with state level agencies. It's free, simple and easy to set up.

Certifications and Contracting with the Government

Federal
Caltrans and Department of Defense (DOD)
www.fedbizoppps.gov

State
Certifications: 8a, Small Disadvantage Business Enterprise
 Disadvantaged Business Enterprise (DBE), Disabled Veteran business Enterprise (DVBE), Small Business Certification
www.sba.gov
www.pd.dgs.ca.gov

LA County
Certification: County Vendor, Minority Business Enterprise (MBE)Women Owned Business Enterprise (WBE)
www.lacounty.gov
http://camisvr.co.la.ca.us/webven
(877) 669-CBES

Apply for DUNS Number
www.dnb.com

Apply for Centralized Contractor Registration (CCR) www.ccr.gov

Obtain NAICS Code
North American Industry Classification System (NAICS)
http://www.sba.gov/sizeNAICS-cover-page.htm

Step 4: *Connecting with Your Customers*

#1

Establishing a P.O. Box

For more than one reason, you would want to establish a postal box for mailing and designation purposes. It is especially wise to have one if you are a home-based business. You don't want consumers appearing on your doorstep.

Post-Office boxes typically cost $35 per month or $165 a year for small boxes.
Advantage: Timely delivery, some postal discounts
Disadvantage: Some creditors and businesses won't send correspondence or merchandise to a P.O. Box.

Postal Connections typically costs $45 quarterly to $140 a year for small boxes.
Advantage: You will receive a box with a street number address, which will not only sound like a street address (as opposed to a P.O. Box), but the box will be available to receive other deliverable merchandise from various carriers. Disadvantage: Have access only during business hours.

#2

Connecting with your customers

You can't get business or make contact with suppliers with out a telephone.
Contact your local telephone provider to establish a business line. Some people choose to use a cell phone for a business line. My recommendation-get a landline. **Why?** When trying to secure credit through Office Suppliers, credit card companies, or in the interest of doing business with more established businesses, a phone line is used to verify your establishment. If they cannot verify the legal status of your company through a landline, there's a great chance you won't get approved. Additionally, a landline with an answering system adds a professional appeal to the business versus having customers call a cell phone.

Think about how you would perceive a business if you called the number provided for the first time and the receiver picked up the call while being in an un-favorable situation/location. Even if you're a consultant, you should have a landline.

#3

Establishing Your Identity

Now it's time to discover who you are and what you represent. As a professional, you want to be recognized as such. At this point, you want to create a logo that fits with your business name.

Your company, and/or product, identity impacts your bottom line. A positive company and product identity enhances your sales and your entire marketing communications plan.

Is Your "Company Identity" The Same As Your "Company Image"

Your company image is how customers, professional associates, the media, and the public at large perceive your business identity.

- **Make a point to notice other company's logos.** Take a stack of magazines and do some easy research. Look at them critically and ask yourself what kind of image they convey and why.
- **Avoid graphics.** Graphic emblems or complex geometric patterns usually don't work for logos. In fact, the simpler and more understated your logo, the more impact it will have. Graphics and patterns will complicate your logo when its purpose is to quickly make a statement about your company or product.
- **Color is a significant element of a logo.** Bright colors are strong attention getters and excite people. Blue and gray are conservative colors. If you want to convey an image that your company is hot, trendy, and on the cutting edge, use red, yellow, and orange. You can use the same color as your competitor uses, but vary the shade to differentiate your business.

For example, American Express uses a consistent typestyle in all of their communications. They employ the same shade of the color green throughout all of their marketing communications involving their basic credit card. The color green is a significant, inseparable aspect of their logo.

- Bold blocks of text invoke the image that the company is strong and large. Italic type can convey a classic or upscale image. Whatever typestyle you choose, it should be simple to read. Once you have a successful combination of color and type, you may then consider embellishing your name with a single, simple graphic element such as a line, border, or box.

For example, The Gap uses a dark box to give great effect in their logo.

Now design your business card, stationery, mailing labels, and envelopes.

13

Step 5: *Introducing Your Business*

#1

Have your business cards printed (minimum of 1,000 cards). Fortunately, there are many options and selections for printing needs.

1) Purchase printing paper for business cards and print them yourself on the computer: $14. (Card stock from Staples, Office Depot, etc. you can also purchase business card paper already pre separated.)
2) Use an independent printer: $30-$100
3) Staples often have great discounts on business cards: $30-$65.

Resource:
1. Heritage Sign Company (Banners, Stationary, Signs, Apparel, etc.)
   Shipping available anywhere
   (661) 266-3300

#2

Create Your Introduction Letter

An introduction letter is the cornerstone of a marketing strategy. This gives you an opportunity to share some important facts about who you are, what you do, and what you're offering. This letter should be kept to a one-page minimum, highlighting key points of your business.

Paragraph #1: The name of your business, the nature of your business, services offered & target market:

_____

_____

_____

_____

Paragraph #2: Product/Service description (What type of product/service do you offer, what are the benefits and features)

_____

_____

_____

_____

Paragraph #3 Introduce you: (Who are you, your position in the company, mission statement)

_____

_____

_____

_____

Paragraph #4: Close with a powerful invitation:
You will have drafted several letters before getting that perfect one. So, have patience. It will come together. Take your time and really think about what important facts you want the reader to know about you and your business. *"First impressions are lasting impressions".*

_____

_____

_____

_____

Note: See Appendix Pg. 70

Step 6: *Database Management*

#1

It's very important and necessary to have a reliable and efficient contact database management system. There's nothing worse than not knowing or having your customer's information stored in manageable order with easy access. Your system should be able to maintain your customer's personal information, business contact information, notes, comments, meeting information, follow-up notification, etc.

At the first stages of business, development costs and expenses become a major factor. Therefore, taking advantage of software programs at your disposal should be utilized.

Approximately, 90% of consumers are using a PC system running Microsoft Office. Should this be you, this would be the opportune time to explore Microsoft Access, which is a "Data Management" program already installed on your computer, and ready to be used. If you're not familiar with the program, take a day to explore its functions. Also, use the "HELP/OFFICE ASSISTANT" to assist you with any questions you may have about a particular process or function.

Access allows you to manage your contacts, keep track of meetings with clients, keep notes, customer's personal information, etc. You can export data from Excel, create fill-in forms, and use many pre-designed templates. **It's a start.**
Remember: Your management system's design should reflect categories according to your business type, and maintain information, which you need to keep track of your transactions and history.

You can also go to www.microsoftofficetemplates.com. Under Templates select Business-Presentations, and you will find an instructional PowerPoint presentation on using Access.

Resource:
1. Microsoft Office: Cost- Free
2. Contact Management-ACT: Cost-$199

Establishing your database

Now that you have created your database, it's time to input your contacts. You should already have collected numerous business cards and met tons of people.

So, let's begin inputting your contact information. Make sure you have all the necessary fields to store your customer's pertinent information, and **don't forget** to include the date and place where you acquired the contact information.

In addition to an internal data management system, you should maintain an external system as well. An external system can be through your email address book. Today, most email providers offer data storing capabilities where you can store contact information, create folders and sub categories, to designate emails to specific groups, and import/export the address book to Excel.

Additionally, one provider in particular -YAHOO! - allows the account holder to create mailing labels directly from an established contact database. Is that cool, or what?

Resources:
1. Directories USA- www.directoriesusa.com
2. Hoovers- www.hoovers.com
3. Manta- www.manta.com

Step 7: *Getting Organized*

#1

<u>Creating forms</u>

Every business must have a system in which to track and keep pertinent information about their clients. At this point you may want to create your basic forms, such as:

1. Client Contact Information Sheet
2. Invoicing
3. Application
4. Contract/Agreement
5. Service Request

Getting organized is one of the most important tasks you will have to ensure the business runs effectively. Being organized in business can have a tremendous effect on your success.

Resource:
1. Forms/Templates- www.officedepot/forms.com
2. Microsoft Office- www.microsofttemplates.com
3. www.entrepreneurassist.com

There is no cost to download and copy these forms.

Step 8: Going Global

#1

<u>Developing your website</u>

Having a website can create many opportunities for your business. In today's business world every business, no matter how small or large, should have a website, which provides consumers (potential customers), creditors, etc. with information on your product/service, the company, and the founder. Additionally, because many consumers are web surfers, having a web site can generate additional revenues and worldwide exposure.

You don't have to go out and find a top notch web master to design and maintain your site, spending hundreds of dollars for a task you can simply do.

First things first!
1. You must decided how the site should be structured
2. What colors would best represent your company
3. How many pages do you need (1,5, or 10)
4. What information will be included on these pages
5. What pictures should be included
6. Who's your target market

There's more to it, however, I am going to provide you with a cost effective solution, which will allow you to create your site at your leisure and save money.

After answering these six questions, you are now ready to develop your site. So what's next!

1. You will need to purchase a domain. There are several domain providers available, thanks to them all, you now have competitive choices. The cheapest I have found is Godaddy.com, however, AT&T has a Merchant Solution package, which offers small businesses a domain name, up to 500 email accounts, shopping cart, store and a store manager. Depending if you have AT & T, this service can be billed to your phone bill, freeing you from additional bills.
2. Because, this is your first website, it is suggested that you consider purchasing a website template. Website templates, depending on where you purchase it from, will give you that professional appeal, exhibiting the look of a quality Webmaster.

Resource:
1. Domain- AT&T (includes email address, domain name, store/cart, website builder, blog) $39 Monthly
2. Website Template- www.allwebcodesigns.com $45-$499
3. MSN- samllbusiness.office.live.com **Free**
4. Yourdomain.com (offer **free** websites and inexpensive registrations)
5. Cheapdomin.com $1.99-$8.99 (offer free website)
6. Blue Media- www.bluegelmedia.com
7. www.templateyes.com
8. Wix – www.wix.com

I highly recommend allwebcodesigns.com templates. It doesn't require any additional software, you don't have to have experience designing a website, it is designed using "Notepad" a program embedded in Microsoft Office and you can maintain the site yourself. Additionally, you can choose from hundreds of templates according to business type. The program, once purchased belongs to you, there are no monthly fees, you are the owner and they have a tech support system, which can walk you through the process.

Step 9: *Organizing Your Office*

#1

Where will you conduct your business? How much space will you need to accommodate your supplies and equipment?

If you are planning on setting up shop in your bedroom (as most home-based start-ups do), you must make sure there's enough walking space, room for a desk, chair, filing cabinet, and some sort of shelving to store books and supplies.

When filing your SE taxes, you can qualify for the Home Office deductions, because you have designated an area of your home to conduct business and perform your administrative duties. No matter what the space size, 1x1, 2x4, or 4x8, you are eligible for home office deductions.

In prior years, the IRS used the room area method to determine how much you can write off as a deduction. Today, all of that has changed. If you are using at least ¼ of the room space in any area of your home, you will qualify.

Supplies needed to organize an effective and professional operational home office:

Printer: Type of business you have and operational needs will determine your printing needs.
1. Create documents, reports, letters, and marketing samples @ 500 sheets per month- HP DeskJet 3500 series
2. Marketing materials, documents, reports, and pictures @ 2500 sheets per month- HP Office jet 6300 series

Laser printers are especially good for mass printing of marketing material with high natural graphics, which need a high resolution for clarity. Lasers are highly recommended for real estate, clothing retailers and graphic artists.

There are many brands and types of printers on the market. Do your part and shop around for the product that best suits your needs.

For cost effective purposes, it would be wise to invest in a 3-in-1 printer that offers printing, scanning, and copying. Purchasing a 3-in-1 will save you hundreds of dollars. The HP 6300 series is a very good model, and has a long life span.

I purchased my 6300 series back in 2004. It's now 2007 and still performing with great quality, just as well as the day I bought it.

Resource:
1. Staples- HP 3500 series: cost $69
2. Staples- HP 6300 series: cost $179

Desk: Select a desk that's suitable for the area, where you will be working. You don't want to purchase an oversized desk that will take up too much space, preventing you from being comfortable and maneuvering around the room. You also want to think about desk color. There are several styles and colors to choose from, however, think about the color scheme in your home. "Your environment is a reflection of our who you are." If you plan on being the next Oprah Winfrey or Donald Trump, think **"BIG."** This doesn't mean you should go out and buy the most expensive desk on the market, but it does mean purchase items that will make you feel like a million dollars. When you sit at your desk, you should feel like the big boss, the next big thing since Wall Street You should feel proud and motivated.

Chair: This is one of the most important items on the list. Yes, a desk is important, because it provides you with a place to get all of those wonderful documents in order, put a beautiful portrait of your family on, and we can't forget about the name plate!

A chair is the one thing that will be keeping you together, while pushing away at the computer all day. Your chair should be as comfortable as possible, with a backrest, tilt action, armrest, and cushioned seat. There's nothing worse than sitting in an uncomfortable chair, causing back pain, muscle tension and squirming.

You can find a nice, low cost leather executive chair fit for an executive.

Resource:
1. Office Max- Executive Chair: Cost $99
2. Office Depot-Executive Chair: Cost $89

#2

Purchase Hardware & Software

Computer: The cost of a new computer will vary depending on the preferred brand and model of your choice. Before purchasing a computer, first think about your needs in terms of mobility.

Will you be using a PC Desktop or Laptop?

If you are a consultant or travel a lot, a laptop may be more suitable than a PC. A laptop provides you with flexibility and mobility. You can work while on the road, in the car, or in the air.

Today, laptops are becoming more popular and affordable. Dell Computers has great deals and will create a software system to suit your business needs. It is not necessary to spend loosely when purchasing a computer. Shop around, and be mindful of advertisements from independent computer retailer's sales of PC's and/or laptops that may be way below market value. If it sounds too good to be true, nine times out of ten, it is.

Whichever system you decide to go with, make sure the operating system is Windows XP. Windows XP is the most widely used system, and offers great functionality and performance.

Software: Your choice of software will be determined by the nature of your business needs. Some businesses require special and specific software.

As an entrepreneur, you're probably strapped for cash and are unable to purchase the latest administrative software. If this is your scenario, then I suggest using the resources and tools Microsoft Office (2000 or higher) has to offer. Microsoft Office has a small business application already included with the software. It's called "Microsoft Office Small Business Tools," and includes Microsoft Direct Mail Manager, Microsoft Business Planning, Microsoft Financial Manager, and Microsoft Small Business Customer Manager. These are the four essential applications needed to build any small business, and help the business owner to get organized.

Microsoft Direct Mail Manager allows you to import databases from Yahoo, Access, Excel or Outlook. You can also verify addresses and zip codes, if you are uncertain of the accuracy, via the Internet, which connects directly to the U.S. Postal Service National Zip Database. It's a great tool to create professional labels and mailings at no additional cost.

Microsoft Business Planning assists entrepreneurs in developing a professional and well thought out business plan. The program will walk you through a series of questions, the answers of which will be automatically applied to the appropriate areas of the business plan. Remember, your plan doesn't have to be 50 pages in length; your plan can be as simple as 25 pages, with well thought-out responses to each question.

Microsoft Financial Manager allows you to create informed decisions about the financial success of your business. You can create financial projections, reports, and analyze the probability of financial growth within the business using the analyzing wizard. This is a great way to learn how to develop and generate financial reports for lenders as well as for your personal reference, and evaluate your business growth over time.

Microsoft Small Business Customer Manager combines your accounting data with Outlook contacts to track and answer key questions about your customer's payment history and services frequently used, as well as creating statements.

This will take approximately one to two days to set up these programs. Take your time and use the Help function should you get lost or need help getting started.

Resource:
Microsoft: Microsoft Small Business Tools- Cost $0

#3

Other supplies to consider

1. A file Cabinet
2. Mailing Labels: Avery or Staples labels are excellent choices. They are standard and inexpensive.
3. Hanging Files: I would recommend using legal size, for that extra length and space. A standard green color would be sufficient and more cost effective.
4. Index Folders: For effective organization, use assorted colors. Designate one color per file type. **Example: workshop-blue, new client-red, schools-green, resources-yellow, etc.** Organizing your files by color will keep you systematic and you will be able to find them easily.
5. File labels: Avery has color-coded file labels; also, clear labels for printing and easy affixing.
6. Pens and Pencils
7. Notepads: Legal
8. Stapler
9. Scissors
10. Dictionary
11. Staples
12. White-out
13. Mini Tape Recorder
14. Paper Clips
15. Rubber Bands
16. Post-Its
17. Stationery
18. USB: External storage to backup and save data
19. Envelopes: White for mailing
20. Envelopes: Gold for large and professional documents
21. Rubber Stamp: Business information
22. Self-Ink Stamps: Completed, Paid, Confidential.

Resources:
Staples
Staples Outlet
Office Max
Office Depot

#1

<u>*Accounting Methods*</u>

For general practices and accurate record keeping, a business owner should invest in a quality "Accounting Software" and a "Dome" bookkeeping recorder.

Microsoft Accounting is an easy-to-use accounting software designed to help the small business owner mange their finances, inventory, and customers.

There are two types of account methods:
1. Cash method
   - Report all income
   - Deduct expenses in the tax year you pay them

2. Accrual method
   - Report income as earned
   - Deduct expenses when you incur them

It's best to decide which accounting method will work best for your business. Whichever method you choose is how you must report your SE taxes.

Cash method accounting is best if you're providing services to consumers or a retailer with a "pay purchase" policy. This means, your customers pay at time of purchase.

- Your income is recorded on the date of purchase, and expenses are deducted for that year as you incur them.

The Accrual method should be used if you are a retailer and offer deferred payment plans to your customers. **Example:** You are in the furniture business and allow your customers to take the merchandise and make monthly payments for an extended period of time.

- Regardless of how many payments are arranged to pay off the balance of the merchandise, when you prepare the sales invoice on that date, this is considered a pay purchase and must be reported to the IRS as earned income for that year. Even if you are not expected to receive payment until the following year, that sale must be reported in the year in which the purchase was made.

Remember to keep track of your expenses daily, and accurately recording your income.

Tax Tips:
1. Keep all of your receipts for three years.
2. Keep a log of your travel, transportation, entertainment, business gifts (you are allowed to write off any gift items purchased for a client).
3. Keep a diary of time and place of business meetings.

Resource:
1. Accounting Software: Microsoft Accounting www.ideawins.com, www.quickbooks.com
2. Favored Bookkeeping Services: 888 425-5560
3. Manual Bookkeeping: Dome Bookkeeping (can be purchased at Staples, Office Depot, Office Max)

Step 11: *Marketing Your Business*

#1

Planning and Marketing

What do we really mean by "marketing?" To many time-starved business owners, marketing means two things: advertising and selling. However, we think that ultimately you'll be more successful if, every so often, you try to look at the "big picture" by taking the time to thoughtfully analyze your products or services and your business as a whole in relation to your competition, your customers, and to societal and regional trends and conditions.

We might say that the key to successful marketing is answering the following question for your business: *How will you communicate a quality and meaningful impression about your business idea (product or service) to the people who might be most interested in buying it?*

There are five questions that should be answered for every business:

- <u>What's unique</u> about your business idea?
- <u>Who is your target buyer</u>? Who buys your product or service now, and who do you really want to sell to?
- <u>Who are your competitors</u>? As a small business, can you effectively compete in your chosen market?
- <u>What positioning message</u> do you want to communicate to your target buyers? How can you position your business or product to let people know they are special, in ways that are important to these buyers?
- <u>What's your distribution strategy</u>? How will you get your product or service in the hands of your customers? Often your distribution method will provide an additional marketing channel, or give you the opportunity to promote more products as you provide the first one.

Whether you sell to consumers or other businesses, you need to identify your potential customers and go after them. Skillful marketing, advertising and PR plans have made small businesses into Fortune companies. There are marketing tools and resources that can help you with marketing material and strategies that will help you promote your business to the market segment you are looking to reach very cost effectively.

The Difference Between a Marketing Plan and a Marketing Campaign

Marketing Plan

A Marketing Plan is a series of collected information from a business plan and research data, which is used to plan and implement a sales pitch for a particular product or service, targeted to a specific group of individuals. This marketing plan consists of planning tools and budgetary information to determine how and when a product or service sales pitch should be made.

Marketing Campaign

A Marketing Campaign is needed to **EXECUTE** the Marketing Plan. It is merely an execution vehicle to put a plan into action. You should know how, where, when and what advertising and marketing segments will be best used to effectively give more exposure to your product or service.

Every new business should have a marketing plan and campaign prepared to launch the introduction of the business as well as the products or services being offered to consumers. Marketing is a vital part of the development and growth of any business. If consumers don't know who you are or what you have to offer, your business becomes an invisible entity, a blind spot in the market place.

Just starting a new business, funds are sometimes limited and scarce. Therefore, keep in mind your marketing plan doesn't have to be elaborate to be effective. With proper budgeting and research, a marketing campaign can be just as effective as a million dollar budget. It's all about strategizing and execution.

Introducing your products/services to the market place

Now comes the fun part, using your creativity. Begin by drafting on a plain sheet of paper, folded in 3 parts (or 2, if you prefer). Outline the structure of your brochure, what sections you want to include, what type of information you want to deliver to the consumer, what color scheme will be used, and whether or not it will be used as a mailer.

Just as a suggestion, when creating your brochure, you may not want to include any costs/pricing, unless the brochure is specifically for the purpose of product/service fees and not information. A separate brochure or cost sheet should be developed, based solely on product/service pricing.

After finalizing the brochure, determine what type of paper would present your product/service in the best light.

For example:
- ➢ if you are a retailer with pictures- Glossy
- ➢ if you provide services- Matte

For cost effective purposes, with a quality printer, you can purchase HP Brochure paper for $30 and produce them yourself at no added expense.

Email Campaign

Distributing announcements, invites, promotions are becoming common and used widely in all industries. It's important to develop an email address book, which can be used to disseminate information about your business.

After creating an Introduction Letter and creating your address book, send each person a copy of the letter via email. Make sure when you send it, to block out the addresses (BCC) of each recipient, to prevent displaying their information. Protect your customer base from potentially being solicited by unauthorized persons.

For a more professional look to your email announcements, you may want to consider using an Email Marketing company. These forms of marketing tools have become popular and are being used widely.

Resource:
1. www.constantcontact.com (Take advantage of the 60 day trial) Cost: $20 Monthly- Unlimited emails
2. Elance- Virtual marketing assistance www.elance.com
3. Virtual Assistance- www.guru.com

Marketing Ideas

Direct Mailing

Flyers
Postcards
Posters
Coupons
Intro Letters

Print Ads

Carwash Ads
Press Release
Local Paper/Magazine

Other Ads

Radio Spots
Bench Ads
Theatre Ads
Cable Ads/Commercial
Church Fans
Bottle Labels

Promotional

Window Wrap
Car Signage
Store Signage
Water Bottle Labels
Stickers
Promotional Items

Other Marketing

Door Tags/Knob Hangers
Website
Newsletter
Write Articles
Website Links
Sponsorship
Create ebook
Social Media

Events

Fundraisers (with NPO)
Product/Service Promotion (Holidays)

Misc. Marketing

Networking
Personable Communication with Customers (via telephone)
Create Partnerships Build Relationship with neighboring businesses

Create Press Release

The purpose of a press release is to gain free exposure through media mediums that are involved in public relations, such as newspaper publications, magazines, radio, television, and Internet.

Press releases are used to inform the public about community events, activities, and business related news. This is a free service and can be submitted to multiple agencies. However, it is not guaranteed that your article will be published. It depends on the following:

1. Time of submission
2. Nature of article
3. Information included in the PR piece
4. How well the PR piece is written
5. Supporting information
6. Community benefit

What to include in a PR piece:
1. No more than 1 page
2. Contact information
3. Date of event
4. An opening line describing the nature of the event
5. Background information about the business owner's experience, any associated credentials to add credibility, etc.
6. How this event/service will benefit the public

Resources:

1. Gale Directory: Cost $500
Another option is to visit your local library and request to view a copy of the Gale Directory. It's the largest publication resource for media and public relations entities, which includes television stations, radio stations, magazines, newspaper publishers, and local community publications nation- wide.

This directory will provide you with not only the names of each entity, but the submission deadlines, contact information, and publication type. Because the publication is so large, it will require a full day's visit to the library. Be sure to take a snack, lunch, water, a pen and notepad, or your laptop.

Note: See Appendix Pg. 75

As a Reference book, the Gale Directory is not available for check out. It can only be viewed in the library.

Media listing and submission:
http://capwiz.com/unausa/dbq/media/?command=state_search&state=ca
Press release submissions: www.pressexposure.com

#3

Create Your Marketing Plan

Marketing Plan

A Marketing Plan is collected information from a business plan, as well as research data, which is used to plan and implement a sales pitch for your product or service. The information is targeted for a specific group of individuals. A marketing plan consists of planning tools and budgetary information to determine how and when a product/service sales pitch should be made.

Your marketing plan should consist of the following information:
Product Description
Target Markets
Competitive Analysis
Collaborative Analysis
Pricing
Promotion (advertising, sales, and customer service)
Production
Distribution
Goals, Responsibilities, Timelines, and Comments/Status
Budget for Marketing and Promotions

Marketing Matrix Strategy

Business owners and managers are responsible for planning and implementing all activities that result in the transfer of goods and services to customers. In planning and implementing strategies there are four basic components "the four P's" of the marketing mix: product, pricing, place, and promotion.

Product-a good, a service, or idea designed to fill a consumer need or want.

Product Differentiation: Promote particular features of products in order to distinguish them in the marketplace and more attractive to consumers.

Pricing-Pricing a product- selecting the best price at which to sell the product. Pricing should cover the varied costs such as operating, administrative, and marketing. Pricing should be attractive, not too high or too low. Successful pricing means finding a profitable middle ground between these two requirements.

Place- Refers to distribution. Company's must make decisions about the best channels through which they distribute products. For example: sell goods to other companies at wholesale cost who in turn distribute them at retail or directly to retailers

Promotion-This is the most visible component of the marketing mix, which are techniques for communicating information about the products. Promotion tools include advertising, personal selling, sales promotions, publicity and public relations.

Promotional Mix

Advertising Media: Consumers will ignore advertising messages that bombard them, they will only pay attention to what interests them. This is why its important to find out who your customers are, which media they pay attention to, what messages appeal to them and how to get their attention.

Television: The most widely used medium of the 25 percent advertising outlays, and reaches a wider audience.

Direct Mail: Accounts for about 20 percent of all advertising outlays, which consists of printed ads mailed directly to consumers. You can select a specific audience and personalize your message.

Newspapers: Account for about 18 percent of all advertising outlays. Like television can reach a wide audience. Keep in mind, like direct mail, news papers too are thrown out after one day. News paper advertisers cannot target a specific audience.

Magazine Ads: Account for approximately 12 percent of all advertising outlays. Magazines have a more attractive benefit. They have long lives and are passed around from one hand to another, which leads to increased exposure over time.

Radio: About 7 percent of all advertising outlays go to radio. Radio ads can be expensive or inexpensive, depending on the time ads are aired. Stations are usually segmented into categories and can be useful to target a specific audience.

Internet: Accounts for about 3 percent of U.S. ad expenditures. You can measure the success of advertisements through electronic tracking.

Outdoor: Outdoor advertising are billboards, signs, ads on buses, and taxis, and subways.

Other: ***Consist of catalogs, tradeshows, handouts***

Sales Promotions

Types of sales promotions are short-term activities designed to encourage consumer buying, which increases the likelihood they will try the product.

Coupons: A certificate to offer savings off regular prices.

Premiums: Free or reduced-priced items.

Point of Sale (POS) Display: Place products at the ends of aisles or near checkout counters, so customers can find your products easier to eliminate competitors.

What promotional mix will you use?

_____

Television:

_____

_____

News Paper:

_____

_____

Radio:

_____

_____

Outdoor:

_____

_____

Direct Mail:

_____

_____

Magazines:

_____

_____

Internet:

_____

_____

Other:

_____

_____

Product Branding

Branding is a process of using symbols to demonstrate the qualities of the product made by a specific company. Brands are designed to signal uniform quality, which consumers can identify the product with its producer.

Then there's brand awareness or brand recognition. Let's take Google for example. When you think about searching the internet what search engine comes to mind. Brand awareness can be very expensive and you must be willing to go all the way. However, there are less expensive ways for gaining brand awareness, product placements and viral marketing. Branding is your best asset.

Product placements are promotional tactics for brand exposure by using characters in television, film, music, magazines, or video games, which are visible to viewers. Products are identified and associated by its unique feature. Law and Order SVU has a distinct dong sound during segment transitions. As a result when a viewer hears this sound they automatically identify it with the television program. Product placements are effective because the message is delivered in an attractive setting that holds the consumer's interest.

Viral Marketing

Viral marketing is another method for increasing brand awareness. It relies on word of mouth and internet presences, which spreads from person to person promoting the usefulness of the product.

Packaging

Packaging can be equally important in its advertising methods, which makes the product attractive. It displays the brand name, and identifies features and benefits.

How will you brand your product?

_____   _____

_____   _____

How will you package your product?

_____   _____

_____   _____

Create Your Marketing Campaign

A Marketing Campaign is a tool used to **EXECUTE** the Marketing Plan. This section requires some strategic thinking on your part to effectively implement the plan and determine how, where, when, and what advertising and marketing mediums will be used.

This section includes:

A SWOT (Strength, Weakness, Opportunity, & Threat analysis)
Business Goals
Tag Line
Timelines
Budget

Note: See Appendix Pg. 50

#4

Create a Press Kit

A press kit is an important marketing tool to have. It can be the ultimate tool that lands you a deal with a prospective client. Press kits are used to compile all of your company's information together in one big package, and should be provided to the media or prospective clients upon request.

A Press Kit includes:
- Your company's history or a description outlining the mission statement, values, and objectives
- Your Bio
- A one sheet
- A 5x7 head-shot picture
- Brochures
- A list of clients
- Letters of endorsement (2-3)
- A competitor comparison chart
- An introduction letter
- A business card
- Any informational fliers and/or press releases of up coming or future events and promotions

Step 12: *Find a Mentor or Form an Advisory Board*

Every entrepreneur is considered a novice in business during the first three years of development. It's impossible to know all there is to know about a business, the industry, and the market place without ever having some kind of experience.

Sometimes a little assistance and advice from an expert (someone who has been in business successfully for more than four years) can educate and walk you through the development stages of starting a business. Having a mentor is especially good, because he/she will share their experiences (good & bad) with you, so you will know how to make conscious decisions beneficial to your business.

You're probably thinking, like most people do, "no one will be willing to take me under their wings and teach me the ropes." That's not true. There are many successful business owners waiting for someone like you to mentor.

How to approach a prospective mentor:
1. Find a business owner you have admired or who is successful in their industry. The person doesn't have to be in your field; in fact, I recommend that you find someone in a totally different industry. Why? Because they won't feel threatened by your entrance into the market as a competitor.
2. Invite them to have lunch on you one day for an hour, to find out more about their business. They will be more than happy to talk about themselves and their success. This is when you take the opportunity to share with them how you admire them. Then mention you are starting a new business and would love to have someone of his or her expertise mentor you. Don't get discouraged if they are unable to make the commitment at that time. Kindly, ask if it would be okay to call on them from time-to-time to seek their advice. Whether they know it or not, that lunch date was the first step to building a long-term relationship which may consist of many more lunch dates and conversations about business.
3. The next day, follow up with a phone call and a thank you note card.

Having a mentor doesn't mean that you have to meet with them on a regular basis. This is a busy world and no one has the time to physically add another meeting to his or her schedule. Therefore, it can be as simple as a 20 minute phone call once a month or staying in contact via email. This process allows a mentor the flexibility to support you, without having to add any additional extended time commitments to their plate.

Resources:
1. Networking organizations
2. Current business owners
3. Churches

38

Step 13: *Start Networking*

One thing to keep in mind is that a business cannot survive on silence. As a business owner, you will want to get the word out about your business, products, and services. Networking is essential to building contacts and relationships with the right people.

Networking with more than one organization would be to your advantage. Utilizing the opportunity to speak before or mingle at the different levels allows you to reach a diverse group of people in various industries.

There are several ways to network: through networking organizations, attending conferences, and the Internet.

The greatest benefit of networking is being affiliated with a networking organization with thousand of members. It's like being a part of a sorority. Members support each other in many ways and sometimes prefer to patronize the services of a fellow member. If a member cannot use your product or service, they will freely and happily refer other people to you. Networking is about business-to-business support and empowering each other to be successful in their endeavor.

I belong to three networking organizations and have increased my business by 75%; 60% are repeat customers, and 45% are a referral base from previous customers -- all from networking.

Attending conferences is another way to physically network amongst professionals and business owners in a professional environment. Visit each booth (if applicable), find out what's what in the business world, who's doing what, and how you can take advantage of these opportunities. Also, collect as many business cards as you can. Find out approximately how many are usually in attendance, and make sure you have enough business cards to hand out.

This is where your determination and ambition are tested. If you are shy and not a people person, this is not the event for you, you may want to consider having someone else to go and represent your business. It's important to be able to strike up a conversation with a stranger and approach anyone.

Using the Internet as a networking tool is becoming very popular. There are more than eight hundred networking opportunities available to small business owners, including networking sites geared toward specific industries and markets.

Networking is the most powerful resource and tool you will ever encounter while in business. Many relationships and ventures are derived from networking.

Preparation:
1. Business cards
2. A developed 30 second elevator speech about your business
3. A warm smile
4. A firm handshake
5. A warm spirit

Networking Resources:

Organizations

1. ABWA (American Business Women's Association) Membership includes Men and Women: Cost-$100 Annually www.abwa.org
2. NAFE (National Association of Female Executives) Membership- Women: Cost-$29 Annually www.nafe.org
3. For You Network/NAFE Affiliate-Membership-Women: Cost-$69 Annually www.foryounetwork.org
4. Million Man Network- Membership Men Only: Cost-$Varies

Social Networking
1. www.startupnation.com
2. www.gobignetwork.com
3. www.entrepreneurship.com
4. www.fraziernet.com
5. www.evancarmichael.com
6. www.entreprenuer.com
7. www.linkedin.com
8. www.facebook.com
9. www.ecademy.com
10. www.speakersite.com

Note: See appendix for additional listings

Other
1. Chambers of Commerce (One in every city)

Step 14: *Find Suppliers*

Now it's time to scout for suppliers. If you are a retailer or your business is product based, do you know who will supply you with inventory or parts?

First decide what products you need and how much inventory is required to get you started. Then begin your search. The Internet is a great resource to find suppliers for your specific product type or industry. Be careful when choosing a supplier. Do your Due-Diligence by researching their site, credentials, and quality of service. Don't go with the first supplier that offers what appears to be the best deal. Check out multiple sites and compare. Your decision should be based on a couple of things.

1. Can you afford what they provide without creating debt?
2. Is this a quality product?
3. Do they offer credit?
4. Can the supplier deliver on demand?

List 5 key pieces of inventory:

1. _____

2. _____

3. _____

4. _____

5. _____

List your 3 key suppliers:

1. _____

2. _____

3. _____

What supplies/inventory will they supply?   What are the delivery terms?

Supplier #1:   Supplier #1:

_____   _____

Supplier #2:   Supplier #2:

_____   _____

Supplier #3:   Supplier #3:

_____   _____

Step 15: *Open Bank Account*

It's crucial to have a separate banking account for your business, rather than using your personal bank account. You will need to manage your business expenses and income apart from your personal affairs, so there won't be any discrepancies when reporting and filing your financial information on your Income Taxes.

Additionally, you want to separate the two so you can better monitor the financial growth of your business. When dealing with suppliers, it is preferred that you pay bills with a company check, and clients typically will prefer to endorse their checks to the business, not the owner. Having a business banking account demonstrates legitimacy and gives clients a sense of sureness.

So, what does it take to open a Business Banking Account?

To open an account for a Sole-Proprietorship, you will need the following:
1. DBA (Fictitious Business Name)
2. EIN (Employer Identification Number)
3. $100

To open an account for an LLC:
1. Articles of Incorporation
2. EIN (Employer Identification Number)
3. Letter of Good Standing from the IRS
4. $100

To open an account for a Corporation:
1. Articles of Incorporation
2. Board Meeting Minutes
3. EIN (Employer Identification Number)
4. Letter of Good Standing from the IRS
5. $100

Appendix Samples

Business Strategy

Detailed Marketing Plan

Simple Marketing Plan

Biography

One Sheet

Introduction Letter

Press Release

Marketing Resources

Business Resources

Strategic Business Plan
for
Business Name

This document comprises a strategic plan for (business) surmise goal, mission, objectives.

Strengths, Weaknesses, Threats & Opportunities

This strategic plan addresses the following key strengths, weaknesses, threats and opportunities, which apply to (business) now and in the foreseeable future:

Strengths:
- #1
- #2
- #3
-

Weaknesses:
- #1
- #2
- #3

Threats: Replace Samples
- Business owner fail to produce accordingly
- Market segment's growth could attract major competition
- Economic slowdown could impede growth and participation
- Market segment's growth could attract major competition
- Competitors attempt to emulate the program

Opportunities: Replace Samples
- Bring community members on board
- Market segment is poised for rapid growth
- Partnerships with local and government agencies
- Partnerships with the Small Business Administration
- Expand to regional areas of the country

Vision

The promoters' vision of (business) in 3-4 year's time is:

Mission Statement

The central purpose and role of (business) is defined as:

Corporate Values

The corporate values governing (business) development will include the following:

- Write in bullet form

Business Objectives

Longer-term business objectives of (Business Name) are summarized as:

- Objective:
- Objective:
- Objective:
- Objective:

Key Strategies

(Business Name) will pursue the following critical strategies:

1. #1
2. #2
3. #3

The following important strategies will also be followed:

1. #1
2. #2
3. #3

Major Goals

(Business Name) will achieve the following key targets over the next 3-4 years:

- Target:
- Target:
- Target:
- Target:

Strategic Action Programs

The following strategic action programs will be implemented:

1. Action:

2. Action:

3. Action:

4. Action:

5. Action:

Monitoring and Evaluation: How will you monitor the effectiveness of your strategy to ensure it is executed and successful.

Write four examples:

1.

2.

3.

4.

Financial Goal:

Year 1: $

Year 2: $

Year 3: $

Year 4: $

Year 5: $

(Company Name)

MARKETING AND PROMOTIONS PLAN

(Product/Program/Service Name)

_____
(Date)

TABLE OF CONTENTS
Product or Services: _____
[Name of product or service]

GENERAL OVERVIEW

Take some time to analyze your company. It's important to know where the company's strength and weaknesses are. This will help you better understand how to market your product (s) and where you will need to improve in order to be competitive in the marketplace.

Let's begin with your **"SWOT"**

Strength: What areas are you most strong in? (customer service, public speaking, management)

Weaknesses: (marketing, retaining customers, cold calling, graphics)

Opportunities: Think about your position in the marketplace, location, environment- what can you do to make it work to your advantage? (add new product to meet market demands, purchase loft next door to expand, institute recycling program for more tax breaks)

Threats: What can prevent your company from growing? (too many competitors in the area, the city moving freeway)

Strength   Weakness

_____   _____

_____   _____

Opportunities   Threats

_____   _____

_____   _____

Demographics: Age (s): _____, _____, _____

Gender: _____, _____

Income Level: _____, _____, _____

Occupation: _____, _____

For business customers:

Industry (s): _____, _____

Location (s):_ _____, _____

Size of firm: (small, medium, large) _____

Example of customer description: The owner of a Motor Cycle shop decided to expand its market niche through mail order catalog for his products. The following is a portion of his customer profile.

Age: 25 to 60 years old

Gender: Men

Marital status: Single or Divorced

Parental status: No children or grown children
Financial profile:
- Income: $25,000 to 85,000 per year
- Investment: Company 401 K
- Debts: $100,000 mortgage; $15,000 car; $2,500 credit cards

Profession: Not important

Buying habits: Prefer o analyze before purchasing motorcycle equipment through mail

order catalog and willing to spend a little more for quality.

Interests: Motorcycling, running, hiking and other outdoor activities.

What is important to him: Personal health, enjoying the outdoors, professional and personal relationships.

Lifestyle: Work 40 to 50 hours per week. Exercise four to five hours per week.

BUSINESS GOALS

Profit: What are your profit goals for the year?

Example: Our current profit goals are: $86,000 post-tax profit
Year Two: $180,000 post-tax profit
Year Three: $396,000 post-tax profit
We have not established any other long-range profit goals at this time.

Current profit goal $_____

Year two $_____

Year three $_____

Sales: What measures will you take to achieve your profit goals?

Example: Our long-term sales goals are to operate at or close to cash flow break-even by Year Two and to be profitable from Year One onward. We would like our profit margin to be 10 percent by Year Three.

_____

_____

_____

Marketing: What additional techniques, services or activities will you implement to condition your company for future growth?

Example: Our long-term marketing goals are to develop an extensive Web site, to increase our public relations activities, and to create additional informative workshops and seminars to draw in new customers.

_____

_____

_____

_____

Product Description (include features and benefits to clients)

Describe the most important features. What is special about it?

1. The design

2. The quality of look

3. Accommodating

4. User friendly

5. Affordable

Features: _____

_____

_____

Describe the benefits. That is, what will the product do for the customer?

1. Safety
2. Healthy
3. More revenue

Benefits: _____

_____

_____

Target Markets (specific groups of customers)

You should identify more than one target market group. Although you may have a primary target market, it is best to have multiple targets, which can create a greater streamline of revenues.

Identify your targeted customers, their characteristics, geographic locations, and

demographics.

Characteristics:

What types of interest should they have?

- Like to play golf

- Like to read

- Outdoor activities

_____

_____

_____

Geographic Location:

- What area will your target market live in?

_____

_____

_____

Reasons the targeted customer will purchase our products: The target customer would purchase motorcycle supplies through our catalog because it is convenient, and we carry a good selection of quality products at the lowest possible prices.

How our products differ from our competitors? Our products are not much different but many of our policies are. We have an earned credit program that allows customers to accrue 5 percent of each purchase in a credit account that they can use at any time and we will match any competitor's catalog price, and we have a 6-month return policy.

POSITION IN THE MARKETPLACE

Description of Our Customers: **Other characteristics you would prefer (See above example of customer characteristics)**

Example: Our customers are 25- to 35-year-old professionals, married or unmarried, without or with children, who are seeking resources to overcome the daily inequities women face in the workplace, home, relationships and with oneself.

_____

_____

_____

_____

Our Customers' Needs: What are some customary needs your market looks for according to industry and market trends.

Example: Our target customers are looking for customized training and informative services that will provide them with all the information necessary to regain control of their lives and deal with personal situations as they arise. Often, they do not have the resources that deals with their issue, so they turn to us for positive and empowering information that promotes self-sufficiency and emotional wellness.

_____

_____

_____

_____

Why Our Customers Choose Us: What makes your company so special that people would want to use your products versus the competition?

Example: Our well-informed, up-to-date consultants, combined with our extensive knowledge of motivational speaking, which addresses women issues, our consultants have first hand experience, we are better-equipped with unique topics and we can relate to the diversifying issues women are faced with daily. Additionally, these qualities allow us to surpass the services provided by other agencies.

_____

_____

_____

_____

What Sets Us Apart From the Competition: How are your products different from your competitors?

Example: What sets our company apart from our competitors- we offer customized workshops for women. We ask them questions, find out exactly what they want and need, and create workshops and seminars to address the appropriate issue.

_____

_____

_____

_____

Competitor Analysis

It is very important to know whom you are competing with in your industry. This section requires you to do your due diligence and research your competitors. To know who they are; what are their practices; how your product (s) measure up to theirs; and their strengths and weaknesses are crucial to strategizing your approach into the marketplace.

Don't take this section lightly- don't take your competitors lightly. The more you know about your competitor the better advantage you will have at gaining customer interest in your product (s).

As a source of reference, visit www.bizequity.com and www.manta.com to find out how much your competitors are worth, when they were established, how many employees the have, their average income and so much more. Also, try google. Google their business, read, review and know their website content, which can be very useful in comparing products and services.

Analyze three competing businesses. (1) Major (2) Equal to your current size and (3) Lesser.

Why? You want to use a major competitor to motivate growth and a lesser to measure your growth.

Note: Product is used interchangeably with service. (product and service are one of the same)

#1 Competitor: _____

Product (s): _____

Common Market(s) That We Serve _____

_____

Product (s) Benefit:

1. _____

2. _____

3. _____

Product Pricing: Are the prices comparable, higher, lower, market rate? (Don't list prices)

_____

Strengths and Weaknesses of Product (s)

S: _____   S: _____

W: _____   W: _____

How does our product (s) compare: _____

_____

_____

What can we do to enhance our product (s)?

_____

_____

_____

#2 Competitor: _____

Product (s): _____

Common Market(s) That We Serve _____

_____

Product (s) Benefit:

1. _____

2. _____

3. _____

Product Pricing: Are the prices comparable, higher, lower, market rate? (Don't list prices)

_____

_____

Strengths and Weaknesses of Product (s)

S: _____   S: _____

W: _____   W: _____

How does our product (s) compare: _____

_____

_____

What can we do to enhance our product (s)?

_____

_____

_____

Marketing Strategy/Campaign

How will you ***Execute*** your marketing plan?

Now that you've created your marketing plan and have identified key areas for promoting your business, it's time to create a campaign strategy, which will put your plan into action. In this section you will need to put on your innovative, creative, and thinking cap to pull this one off.

THINK BIG
THINK SMART
THINK SAVVY

Putting Your Strategy Into Action

MARKETING CAMPAIGN SPECIFICS

Goals of the Campaign:

Example: We would like to increase our visibility, attract new customers, and display special offers that are currently available.

_____

_____

_____

Campaign Focus: Specific Services or General Promotion?

Example: Our primary focus is to expand our customer base. We would also like to keep our current customers aware of special promotions and workshops we are offering and secure their future business with us.

_____

_____

_____

Product (s) to be Advertised: What specific product(s) do you want to give emphasis to?

Example: We will be advertising our complete range of workshops and seminars, services, and special discounts on corporate packages.

_____

_____

_____

Measurements of Success: How will you determine how successful your campaign and planning efforts were?

Example: We will measure the ad campaign's success by the number of inquiries received after its launch. This includes phone inquiries as well as inquiries made via website and email.

_____

_____

_____

_____

Evaluation of Effectiveness: What method will you use to monitor the campaigns effectiveness?

Example: We review and track the campaign's effectiveness beginning one month after its launch. We will evaluate its effectiveness based on the number of inquires we receive and any corresponding increase in revenue.

_____

_____

_____

_____

Length of Campaign
Example: This campaign will run through December, for a total of four months.

Start Date: _____

End Date: _____

BUDGET

Your budget is very crucial in deciding what advertising segments to use and how often you should use them. It should be a realistic budget, one that corresponds with your business plan financial goals, cash flow and profit & loss statements.

Annual Marketing Budget
What is your annual Marketing budget? $_____

Budget For This Campaign: What is the amount allocated for this particular campaign?

Example: $4,000. This includes $200 for Web site and database design, implementation, and material production, which will be useful for future campaigns and media coverage.

$_____

Which includes:

_____   _____

_____   _____

Simple Marketing Plan

Start: _____ End: _____

Sales Goal: $ _____

Campaign Slogan: _____

Situation Analysis:

Competitors:
    1. _____

    2. _____

Product Benefit & Features: (Features are characteristics of a product; Benefits are the value of a product)

    1. _____

    2. _____

    3. _____

Target Audience: _____

Demographics:

Age Group: _____

Education Level: _____

Household Income: _____

Culture: _____

Other: _____

Location: _____, _____,

Business Customers:

Budget Size: _____ No. Employees _____

Business Type: _____

Location: _____ _____

Goals for this campaign:

1. _____

2. _____

3. _____

4. _____

Strategy

Marketing Activities: Timeline:

1. _____   _____

2. _____   _____

3. _____   _____

4. _____   _____

What media segments will be used?

1. _____   _____

2. _____   _____

3. _____   _____

4. _____

Resources:

Advertising: _____, _____

_____, _____

_____, _____

Other: _____, _____

_____, _____

_____, _____

Biography

A biography should include the following information and not exceed one page. Each paragraph may vary in length.

Paragraph one: This is your introduction section.

- Your name and title with company
- Name of company
- Company's mission and purpose
- Briefly give examples of your accomplishments

Paragraph two: More details on your accomplishments.

- Great details about your accomplishments
- Indicate any experience relevant to position or nature of business

Paragraph three: Community services, special projects

- Outstanding works with other organizations or service agencies
- Your purpose with in the organizations
- Indicate any book writings, published articles, etc.

Paragraph four:

- Indicate any organizational memberships, club affiliations

Paragraph five:

- Briefly list your education background
- List any degrees

Paragraph six: Closing.

Indicate your life's purpose and overall goals.

One Sheet

A one sheet is exactly that, one sheet of paper with creditable information about you and your services/products. This is a very powerful sheet of paper. It carries a lot of weight with potential customers, especially if you are considering marketing to businesses. This one sheet of paper sums up who you are, what you do, who your clients are and how they perceive both you and your product/services.

A One Sheet includes the following information. The format may vary according to the nature of your business and your target market. Keep in mind, no matter what format you choose, always include a head-shot picture of yourself with your company's logo.

- A picture
- Your logo
- List 7-10 clients
- Include at least five testimonials from clients
- List your products/services

Sample Introduction Letter

Sahra Milstone
Director of Sales
125 Whale Rd.
Sweatland, Ohio 56325

May 29, 2003

Jack Nelson
Production Manager
12546 S. Corn Ave.
Sweatland, Ohio 56325

Dear Mr. Nelson,

Towne Bank is pleased to announce new services for small business owners. We specialize in expert financial planning and asset management. Our goal is to help you find better ways to manage your cash flow. We offer insurance coverage and can guide you in tax and other accounting services. Our on-line services allow customers to check deposit and loan amounts 24 hours a day.

Whether you are starting or expanding your business, Towne bankers are here to help you. Towne Bank is committed to providing superior service at affordable rates.

Towne Bank is open from 8:30 a.m. to 5:30 p.m., Monday through Saturday. On Tuesday and Thursday evenings, we are open until 7 p.m. for the convenience of small business customers. For more information, call 123-456-7890.

Sincerely,

Sahra Milestone
Director of Sales

The Company

Founded in 2003, the Company is specialized in transaction processing and book keeping for offshore clients. DCJ & Company is an accounting and bookkeeping services company that utilizes the Internet to facilitate communications and document transfers, enabling clients to benefit from outsourcing while receiving professional services at an affordable rate.

II.   *Vision Statement*

Highly personalized service and accommodating the needs of clients has always been the hallmark of our business. It is our vision to be a stand out even more as the best managed and most professionally operated book keeping service provider. In a highly competitive industry, we intend to distinguish ourselves by planning our services very carefully; having specific standards for servicing the clients; and carefully monitoring the quality of our service. We are also going to carefully communicate the key differences and advantages in doing business with us, whereby clients are aware that we provide the most innovative products and consistency through quality service.

Mission Statement

Competitive nature of today's business has posed the greatest challenge to all the corporate – availability of quality resource at a reasonable price. We at DCJ & Company offer innovative and yet practical solutions to comprehend the needs of the client for book keeping and accounting. Our mission is to be a pioneer and leader in the outsourced bookkeeping and accounting industry.

Why should you outsource?

➢ Because your business is growing exponentially but your resources can't cope with the growth.

➢ Because you'd rather focus on mission-critical issues and not interested in frittering away time and energy on non-core functions.

> Because you need the best talent in the world, but it's scarce/out of reach/ just not available in your country.
> Because you need a professional accountant to take care of one of the major support functions of your organization.

In today's globalize and networked economy, outsourcing has never been so easy or made so much business sense. The question is not "Why outsource?" but rather, "Why not?"

Benefits of Outsourcing

> Reduce overheads, free up resources
> Avoid capital expenditure like purchase of hardware and software
> Improve efficiency
> Offload non-core functions and concentrate on your own business
> Get access to specialized skills
> Save on manpower and training costs
> Reduce operating costs
> Improve speed and service
> Establish long-term, strategic relationships with world-class service providers to gain a competitive edge
> Enhance tactical and strategic advantages
> Spread your risks
> Benefit from the provider's expertise in solving problems for a variety of clients with similar requirements.

> Leverage the provider's extensive investments in technology, methodologies and people
> Provide value-added services
> Avoid the cost of chasing technology
> Obtain needed project management and implementation consulting expertise, along with access to best practices and proven methodologies
> Provide the best quality services, products and people
> Be reliable and innovative

Our Services

At DCJ & Company we do not just offer a range of book keeping services, but will also forge a productive business relationship with our clients. Our solutions are customized to meet client's needs. In addition to world-class bookkeeping services DCJ & Company will also strive to bring gains in productivity to the client.

These are the range of bookkeeping services that DCJ & Company offer:

➢ Document Management
➢ General Ledger Entries
➢ Accounts Receivables
➢ Accounts Payables
➢ Reconciliation (Bank statement, Debtor's, Creditor's)
➢ Depreciation
➢ Balancing of Books
➢ Migration of legacy systems
➢ Financial Reports
➢ Assist the Client to raise funds from banks
➢ Preparing financial projections and business plan
➢ Medical Billing
➢ Marketing services to generate traffic to a website. Note: We provide posting services on free classified sites in US (Craigslist) and do not provide SEO and SEM services at present.

Our Team

Strong Management team with a combination of business and technical know how is a key strength of DCJ & Company. Mary, a Masters in Commerce is well versed in Accounting and Book Keeping with 5 years of experience in the field of accounting. She as the Operational Manager drives the execution and monitors the quality of service.

Rania Mosses is a specialist consultant for DCJ & Company and leads the business development initiatives. Rania brings in experience from varied industries and being a professional Public Accountant and a member of Institute of Chartered Accountants of Columbia, she has 15 years of experience in book keeping and business consulting. Harish is also a Certified IT auditor (CISA, IL, USA) and has worked as a Senior Auditor at PricewaterHouse Coopers, in the Republic of Maldives and a Big4 Consulting firm in India. He has got extensive knowledge in preparation of business plan and financial projections and financial analysis. He has forged close relationships with key customers and is highly regarded by the employees throughout our organization.

Jason McNally is a business consultant for DCJ & Company who brings rich experience in business process especially in Medical Billing and related business. He is a talented executive with deep knowledge of the Medical Billing industry and specific expertise on 16 Medical Billing software commonly used by the national Health Care industry.

Gery Katz, a Masters in Commerce and a Certified Public Accountant has extensive technical skills to deliver value to our book keeping service. He has 23 years of book keeping and auditing experience and is a member of Institute of CPA Association.

Contact Information
DCJ & Company
124 s. Avery Port
Jacent, Michigan 34509
Phone: 313 229-3000
Website: www.DCJ & Company.com
Email: djadmin@dcjandcom.com

We look forward to serve your business needs.

Contact: Connie Sparks
26873 Sierra Hwy, Ste.138
Santa Clarita, CA 91321
(661) 298-7126

PRESS RELEASE

The Success Keys to Starting a Business

The Wade Institute, LLC & Microsoft Accounting
Partnering to Strengthen Communities, Building Small Businesses

The Wade Institute, LLC and Microsoft Accounting Professional have partnered to bring free small business seminars to local communities throughout Los Angeles County. The first of many will take place on Saturday September 15th to be held at US Bank in Los Angeles. The Wade Institute, LLC is a Small Business Development Company, founded by Connie Sparks a consultant to Micro-Enterprises. Ms. Sparks is committed to educating women in business and those transitioning from corporate America to Entrepreneurship. It has been her life's mission to play an intricate role in the development of our economy, communities, and families, creating more profitable businesses, and jobs. To-date she has taught more than 2000 entrepreneurs and small business owners collectively throughout the Los Angeles and Glendale County areas alone. Her entrepreneurship seminars and workshops have become increasingly popular among the SBA/Small Business Development Center in Santa Clarita, CA and various colleges throughout Southern California. In addition to her commitment to educate women in business, she is one of few consultants in California to serve as an intermediary for one of SBA's Small Business Loan programs (Community Express/SOHO), which is not offered by any traditional lender. Her role as a Technical Advisor to the program is to encourage women in business who primarily have a Home Office or has been in business under a year and require no more than $25,000 in capital, to take advantage of this opportunity. Intrigued by Ms. Sparks and her commitment, Microsoft Accounting an extension of Microsoft Software, recognized her efforts in reaching out to inner city communities and proposed to join forces to offer additional resources in business accounting. MSA has developed an accounting software suitable and affordable for the average small business owner. The product is designed to provide its user with the essential accounting needs necessary to effectively manage the day-to-day functions of self-financial management. This partnership is the beginning of a new wave of small business products and services delivered to entrepreneurs through seminars and workshops.

The event will take place on September 15, 2007, US Bank located at 5760 Crenshaw Blvd., Los Angeles, Ca. For registration information call Connie Sparks at (661) 298-7126 or email csparks@wadeinstitute.org. You may also visit our website www.wadeinstitute.org.

####

Components of a News Release

FOR IMMEDIATE RELEASE
These words should appear in the upper left-hand margin with all letters capitalized.

Headline
This should be a sentence that gives the essence of what the press release is about. Articles, prepositions, conjunctions of three letter words or fewer should be lowercased.

Dateline
This should be the city your press release is issued from and the date you are mailing your release.

Lead Paragraph
A strong introductory paragraph should grasp the reader's attention and should contain the information most relevant to your message such as the five W's (who, what, when, where, why). This paragraph should summarize the press release and include a hook to get your audience interested in reading more.

Body
The main body of your press release is where your message should fully develop. Many companies choose to use a strategy called the inverted pyramid, which is written with the most important information and quotes first.

Company Boilerplate
Your press release should end with a short paragraph that describes your company, products, service and a short company history. If you are filing a joint press release include a boilerplate for both companies.

Contact Information
Name, Phone, Email

Free Press Release and Event Listings

- 1888PressRelease.com
- 24-7 Press Release
- AddPR.com
- BizEurope.com
- eCommWire.com
- Express-Press-Release.com
- Free-News-Release.com
- Free-Press-Release.com
- Free-Press-Release-Center.info
- FreePressIndex.com
- FreePressRelease.co.cc
- FreePressReleases.co.uk
- i-Newswire.com
- IndiaPRWire.com
- MediaSyndicate.com
- MyFreePR.com
- NewswireToday.com
- PageRelease.com
- PR.com
- PR9.net
- PR-Inside.com
- PRCompass.com
- PRlog.com
- PRurgent.com
- PRzoom.com
- PressAbout.com
- PressBox.co.uk
- PressFlow.co.uk
- PressMethod.com
- PressRelease.com
- PressReleasePoint.com
- TechPRSpider.com
- TheOpenPress.com

Events

www.Blacknla.com

Churches

SCV Website (www.santa-clarita.com)

www.MySantaClarita.com

www.NAFE.com

www.Meeting&Mixers.com

www.SaveTheDateCentral.com

Latimes.com/submit (Entertainment only)

Laweekly.com (Entertainment only)

KHTS www.hometownstation.com

Santa Clarita Signal (lifestyle@the-signal.com)

SCV Business Journal (lifestyle@the-signal.com)

www.Blackwomenconnect.com

San Fernando Valley Business Journal (editor@sfvbj.com or fax 818 676-1747)

Santa Clarita Guide (Calendar@santaclaritaguide.com-submit 3weeks prior to event) or call 661 297-2918

Walmart LCD Screens (susan.schanz@santaclaritaguide.com- submit 3 weeks prior to event)

Resources

Online Networking

Sites proved entrepreneurial advice, free marketing ad placements, and national exposure.
www.supernation.com
www.entrepreneur.com
www.startupnation.com
www.twitter.com
www.allcities.org
www.speakerssite.com
www.ceospace.net
www.empoweredwoman.com
www.speakerslead.com
www.ecademy.com

Website Templates

www.alwebcodesigns.com
www.besttemplatedesign.com
www.easytemplates.com

Marketing

PR News Wire provides national press release services (Estelle Seals (201) 360-6572)
www.prnewswire.com

Carwash Advertising
(800) 469-120

National Cinemedia: Movie Theatre Advertising
(323) 661-3746

www.bttradespace.com

www.myquire.com

Sales Leads
www.directoriesusa.com

Stock Photo for Marketing Material
www.istockphoto.com

Post Press Releases
www.Ezinearticles.com

http://capwiz.com/unausa/dbq/media/?command=state_search&state=ca
www.pressexposure.com

ebook distributor
www.issuu.com
www.desktopauthor.com

Association for Progressive Communications offers Mission-Driven Business Planning Toolkit. This is a free web-based resource that includes a forms-driven market analysis approach and how to develop a marketing plan.
www.apc.org/english/ngos/business/busplan/mtoolkit.htm

InfoUSA lists more than 14 million businesses and 200 million consumers and 104 million households in its database. You can create a customized list of businesses or residents pertaining to geography, demographics and sales figures, you can also purchase a lists of new homeowners. Searching the database is free.
www.infousa.com

Inc.com-Market Research has a collection of articles about market research, including low-budget suggestions for conducting your own market research.
www.inc.com/guides/marketing/24018.html

MarketResearch.com is a searchable database of market research reports coving all industry sectors, both domestic and international. The site offers free searching abstracts, and tables of contents, the searchable information are good for periodical quotes.
www.marketresearch.com

Biz Journals offers recent news from more than 40 local business journals. You can search and view articles by topic, industry, or market location. This site is particularly helpful when gathering comparison industry data.
www.bizjournals.com/

Research
EconData.Net provides comprehensive socioeconomic (demographics, income, output and trade) data sources.
www.econdata.net

Economic Statistics Briefing Room provides links to economic information produced by Federal agencies on employment, income, international trade, money, output, prices, production, transportation and social stats.
www.whitehous.gov/fsbr/esbr.html

FedStats offers statistics from over 100 U.S. Federal agencies with links to stats on geography, and other United States Metropolitan Area Data Book.
www.fedstats.gov

National Center for Health Statistics is the Federal Government's principal vital and health statistics agency. It includes healthcare trends and health insurance coverage.
www.cdc.gov/nchs/

U.S. Census Bureau Economic Programs provides economic stat by geography, sector, and frequency. This site also profiles American business every five years, from the national to local level, which includes business patterns, e-commerce, foreign trade, monthly wholesale and retail trade.
www.census.gov/econ/www/

Virtual Office Space
The Metropolitan Business Center
Lancaster, CA
(661) 874-4333

Barrister Suite
Valencia, CA
(661) 362-0700

Virtual Assistance
www.elance.com
www.guru.com

Virtual Receptionist
www.answeramerica.com

Free PDF Creator-Doc Conversion
www.pdf995.com

Online Conference Meetings
www.webexcommunication.con
www.gotomeeting.com
www.instantconference.com